Perry Clement

Calm and Confident

A Teen's Guide to Managing Anxiety

For my mum, who never stopped believing in me.

Chapter 1: Understanding Anxiety

What is Anxiety?

Anxiety is a common emotion that everyone experiences at some point in their lives. It is a natural response to stress or fear, and can manifest in a variety of ways. For some, anxiety may be a mild feeling of nervousness or worry, while for others it can be overwhelming and debilitating. Understanding what anxiety is and how it affects you is the first step in learning how to manage it effectively.

In simple terms, anxiety is your body's way of preparing you to deal with a perceived threat. When you feel anxious, your body releases stress hormones like adrenaline, which can trigger the "fight or flight" response. This response is designed to help you react quickly to danger, but when anxiety becomes chronic or excessive, it can interfere with your ability to function normally.

There are many different types of anxiety disorders, including generalized anxiety disorder, social anxiety, and panic disorder. Each type of anxiety can have its own set of symptoms and triggers, but they all share the common theme of excessive worry and fear. It's important to remember that anxiety is a real and valid mental health issue, and seeking help is nothing to be ashamed of.

Teens are particularly vulnerable to anxiety due to the many changes and pressures they face during this stage of life. Academic stress, social pressures, and hormonal changes can all contribute to feelings of anxiety. Parents play a crucial role in helping their teens manage anxiety by providing a supportive and understanding environment, and encouraging open communication about their feelings.

Learning to recognize the signs of anxiety and developing healthy coping mechanisms is key to managing anxiety effectively. This may involve practicing relaxation techniques, seeking therapy or counseling, and making lifestyle changes to reduce stress. By taking proactive steps to address anxiety, teens can learn to navigate their emotions and build resilience for the future. Remember, you are not alone in your struggles with anxiety, and there are resources and support available to help you through it.

Common Symptoms of Anxiety

Anxiety is a common experience for many people, especially in the teenage years. It's important to recognize the symptoms of anxiety so that you can address them and manage your feelings effectively. In this subchapter, we will discuss some of the most common symptoms of anxiety that teens may experience.

One of the most common symptoms of anxiety is excessive worry or fear about a variety of situations. This worry can be overwhelming and can make it difficult to focus on everyday tasks. Teens with anxiety may find themselves constantly thinking about the worst-case scenario in any given situation, leading to increased stress and tension.

Physical symptoms of anxiety can also manifest in teens. These symptoms may include rapid heartbeat, shortness of breath, sweating, and trembling. These physical sensations can be frightening and may exacerbate feelings of anxiety. It's important for teens to recognize when their physical symptoms are related to anxiety so that they can use coping strategies to manage them effectively.

Teens with anxiety may also experience difficulties with sleep. Insomnia, nightmares, and restless sleep are common issues for those struggling with anxiety. Lack of quality sleep can further exacerbate anxiety symptoms, creating a vicious cycle that can be difficult to break. It's important for teens to prioritize good sleep hygiene and relaxation techniques to improve their overall well-being.

Another common symptom of anxiety in teens is avoidance behavior. Teens may avoid certain situations or activities that trigger their anxiety, leading to social isolation and missed opportunities for growth and development. It's important for teens to challenge themselves and gradually face their fears in order to overcome anxiety and build confidence in their abilities.

Overall, recognizing and understanding the common symptoms of anxiety is the first step in effectively managing this challenging condition. By learning how to identify and address anxiety symptoms, teens can develop healthy coping strategies and build resilience in the face of stress and uncertainty. With the right tools and support, teens can learn to navigate their anxiety and cultivate a sense of calm and confidence in their daily lives.

Causes of Anxiety in Teens

Anxiety is a common experience for many teens, and there are various factors that can contribute to the development of anxiety in adolescents. One of the main causes of anxiety in teens is academic pressure. With the pressure to excel in school, meet high expectations, and secure a bright future, many teens experience overwhelming stress and anxiety about their academic performance. This can lead to feelings of inadequacy, fear of failure, and constant worry about the future.

Another common cause of anxiety in teens is social pressures. Adolescence is a time of significant social development, and teens often feel pressure to fit in, be liked, and maintain friendships. Social media also plays a role in increasing social pressures, as teens compare themselves to others and feel the need to constantly present a perfect image online. This can lead to feelings of insecurity, loneliness, and anxiety about social interactions.

Family dynamics can also contribute to anxiety in teens. Conflict within the family, high expectations from parents, and lack of support can all create a stressful home environment that can impact a teen's mental health. Additionally, traumatic events such as divorce, death in the family, or abuse can cause significant emotional distress and lead to anxiety in teens.

Genetics and biology also play a role in the development of anxiety in teens. Some individuals may have a genetic predisposition to anxiety disorders, making them more susceptible to experiencing anxiety in response to stressors. Imbalances in neurotransmitters, such as serotonin and dopamine, can also contribute to the development of anxiety disorders in teens.

Finally, societal factors such as pressure to succeed, fear of the unknown, and uncertainty about the future can all contribute to anxiety in teens. The constant barrage of information and expectations from society can create a sense of overwhelm and fear of not measuring up. It's important for teens and parents to recognize these causes of anxiety and work together to address them in a healthy and effective way. By understanding the root causes of anxiety in teens, we can better support them in managing their anxiety and promoting their mental well-being.

Chapter 2: The Impact of Anxiety

How Anxiety Affects Teens

Anxiety is a common emotion experienced by teens, but when it becomes overwhelming, it can have a significant impact on their daily lives. In this subchapter, we will explore how anxiety affects teens and offer strategies for managing and coping with these feelings. It is important for both teens and parents to understand the effects of anxiety so they can work together to find solutions that work best for each individual.

One way that anxiety affects teens is through physical symptoms. When someone is anxious, their body goes into fight or flight mode, which can lead to increased heart rate, sweating, and muscle tension. These physical symptoms can be uncomfortable and can make it difficult for teens to focus on everyday tasks. By recognizing these symptoms, teens can learn to identify when they are feeling anxious and take steps to calm themselves down.

Another way that anxiety affects teens is through their mental health. Anxiety can lead to feelings of worry, fear, and self-doubt, which can impact a teen's self-esteem and confidence. This can also lead to difficulty concentrating, memory problems, and trouble sleeping. By addressing these mental health symptoms, teens can learn to reframe their negative thoughts and develop coping strategies to manage their anxiety more effectively.

Socially, anxiety can also have a significant impact on teens. It can lead to feelings of isolation, difficulty making friends, and avoidance of social situations. This can further perpetuate feelings of anxiety and make it harder for teens to break out of this cycle. By seeking support from friends, family, or mental health professionals, teens can learn to navigate social situations with more confidence and build stronger connections with others.

In conclusion, it is important for teens and parents to recognize the ways in which anxiety can affect teens and work together to find effective strategies for managing and coping with these feelings. By addressing physical, mental, and social symptoms of anxiety, teens can learn to navigate their emotions more effectively and build resilience in the face of challenges. With the right support and resources, teens can learn to feel calm and confident in managing their anxiety.

The Importance of Managing Anxiety

Anxiety is a common experience for both teens and adults, but it can be especially challenging for teenagers who are navigating the pressures of school, friendships, and figuring out their place in the world. In this subchapter, we will explore the importance of managing anxiety and provide some strategies for teens to cope with their anxious thoughts and feelings.

Managing anxiety is crucial for maintaining good mental health and overall well-being. When left unchecked, anxiety can have a significant impact on a teen's daily life, leading to difficulty concentrating, disrupted sleep patterns, and even physical symptoms such as headaches or stomachaches. By learning how to manage their anxiety, teens can improve their resilience and ability to cope with stressors that come their way.

One of the key reasons why managing anxiety is important for teens is that it can help them build confidence and self-esteem. When teens are able to effectively cope with their anxious thoughts and feelings, they can feel more in control of their emotions and better equipped to handle challenging situations. This can lead to increased self-confidence and a greater sense of self-worth, which are essential for navigating the ups and downs of adolescence.

In addition to improving mental health and self-esteem, managing anxiety can also have positive effects on a teen's physical health. Chronic anxiety can take a toll on the body, leading to increased levels of stress hormones and potential long-term health consequences. By learning how to manage anxiety through techniques such as mindfulness, deep breathing, or talking to a trusted adult, teens can reduce the physical toll that anxiety takes on their bodies and improve their overall health and well-being.

Overall, the importance of managing anxiety cannot be overstated for teens. By developing healthy coping mechanisms and seeking support when needed, teens can learn to navigate the challenges of adolescence with greater ease and confidence. In the following chapters, we will explore a variety of strategies and techniques that teens can use to manage their anxiety and build a sense of calm and confidence in their lives.

The Connection Between Anxiety and Mental Health

Anxiety is a common experience for many teens, but it can have a significant impact on mental health if not properly managed. In this subchapter, we will explore the connection between anxiety and mental health, and how understanding this relationship can help teens and parents better navigate the challenges of anxiety.

One of the key aspects of the connection between anxiety and mental health is the way in which anxiety can exacerbate existing mental health issues. For example, teens who already struggle with depression or other mental health conditions may find that their symptoms worsen when anxiety is present. This is because anxiety can trigger a range of negative emotions and thoughts, making it difficult to cope with the challenges of daily life.

Additionally, anxiety can also lead to physical symptoms that impact mental health. For example, chronic anxiety can lead to sleep disturbances, digestive issues, and headaches, all of which can contribute to feelings of stress and overwhelm. These physical symptoms can further exacerbate mental health issues, creating a cycle of anxiety and poor mental health that is difficult to break.

Furthermore, the way in which teens cope with anxiety can also impact their mental health. For example, some teens may turn to unhealthy coping mechanisms such as substance abuse or self-harm in an attempt to manage their anxiety. These behaviors can have serious long-term consequences for mental health, making it essential for teens and parents to seek healthy coping strategies for managing anxiety.

By understanding the connection between anxiety and mental health, teens and parents can work together to develop effective strategies for managing anxiety and promoting positive mental health. This may include therapy, medication, lifestyle changes, and other interventions that can help teens build resilience and cope with anxiety in a healthy way. By taking a proactive approach to anxiety management, teens can improve their mental health and overall well-being.

Chapter 3: Techniques for Managing Anxiety

Deep Breathing Exercises

Deep breathing exercises are a powerful tool in managing anxiety and promoting relaxation. When we are stressed or anxious, our breathing tends to become shallow and rapid, which can exacerbate our feelings of panic. By practicing deep breathing exercises, we can effectively calm our nervous system and bring ourselves back to a state of calm and balance.

One simple deep breathing exercise that you can try is called the 4-7-8 technique. Start by inhaling slowly through your nose for a count of 4, hold your breath for a count of 7, and then exhale slowly through your mouth for a count of 8. Repeat this cycle several times, focusing on the sensation of your breath entering and leaving your body. This exercise can help to slow down your heart rate and relax your muscles, making it easier to cope with feelings of anxiety.

Another effective deep breathing exercise is belly breathing. This technique involves breathing deeply into your diaphragm, allowing your belly to rise as you inhale and fall as you exhale. By focusing on breathing deeply into your belly, you can activate your body's relaxation response and reduce feelings of tension and stress. Practice belly breathing regularly to build a sense of calm and resilience in the face of anxiety.

Deep breathing exercises are not only beneficial for managing anxiety in the moment, but they can also help to build your overall resilience to stress over time. By incorporating deep breathing exercises into your daily routine, you can train your body and mind to respond more effectively to stressful situations, reducing the frequency and intensity of anxiety symptoms. Consistent practice is key, so try to set aside a few minutes each day to engage in deep breathing exercises and reap the benefits of a calmer and more confident mindset.

Teens and parents alike can benefit from incorporating deep breathing exercises into their anxiety management toolkit. By learning to harness the power of your breath, you can take control of your anxiety and cultivate a sense of calm and confidence in the face of life's challenges. Whether you are feeling overwhelmed by schoolwork, social pressures, or everyday stressors, deep breathing exercises offer a simple yet effective way to ground yourself in the present moment and find peace amidst the chaos. So take a deep breath, exhale slowly, and embrace the power of deep breathing to guide you towards a calmer and more confident state of being.

Mindfulness and Meditation

Mindfulness and meditation are powerful tools that can help teens manage anxiety and stress. By practicing mindfulness, teens can learn to focus on the present moment and let go of worries about the past or future. Meditation, on the other hand, can help teens quiet their minds and cultivate a sense of inner peace. Together, these practices can help teens develop a greater sense of calm and confidence in the face of anxiety.

One of the key benefits of mindfulness and meditation is their ability to help teens become more aware of their thoughts and emotions. By paying attention to their thoughts without judgment, teens can learn to recognize when they are feeling anxious and take steps to calm themselves down. This increased self-awareness can also help teens identify triggers for their anxiety and develop strategies for managing them.

In addition to helping teens manage anxiety, mindfulness and meditation can also improve their overall well-being. Research has shown that these practices can reduce symptoms of depression, improve sleep quality, and enhance cognitive function. By incorporating mindfulness and meditation into their daily routine, teens can experience a wide range of physical and mental health benefits.

For parents, encouraging their teens to practice mindfulness and meditation can be a proactive way to support their mental health. By modeling these practices themselves and creating a supportive environment for their teens to explore mindfulness and meditation, parents can help their teens develop healthy coping mechanisms for managing anxiety. Additionally, parents can work with their teens to find resources and guidance on how to incorporate mindfulness and meditation into their daily routine.

Overall, mindfulness and meditation are valuable tools for teens to manage anxiety and cultivate a sense of calm and confidence. By incorporating these practices into their daily routine, teens can develop greater self-awareness, improve their overall well-being, and build resilience in the face of stress and anxiety. With the support of parents and guidance from mental health professionals, teens can harness the power of mindfulness and meditation to navigate the challenges of adolescence with grace and strength.

Physical Activity and Exercise

Physical activity and exercise play a crucial role in managing anxiety and improving mental health. When we engage in physical activity, our bodies release endorphins, which are often referred to as "feel-good" hormones. These endorphins help to reduce feelings of stress and anxiety, promoting a sense of well-being and relaxation. Regular exercise can also help to improve sleep quality, boost self-esteem, and increase energy levels, all of which are important factors in managing anxiety.

For teens struggling with anxiety, finding ways to incorporate physical activity into their daily routine can be incredibly beneficial. Whether it's going for a run, practicing yoga, or playing a team sport, getting moving can help to alleviate symptoms of anxiety and improve overall mental health. Encouraging your teen to find an activity they enjoy and can commit to regularly can make a significant difference in their anxiety management.

As a parent, it's important to support and encourage your teen in their efforts to stay active. This may involve helping them find activities they enjoy, creating a schedule that allows for regular exercise, or even joining them in physical activities when possible. By modeling healthy behaviors and emphasizing the importance of physical activity, you can help your teen develop lifelong habits that promote good mental health and well-being.

It's also important to remember that physical activity doesn't have to be intense or time-consuming to be effective. Even short bursts of activity, such as taking a walk around the block or doing a quick workout at home, can help to reduce feelings of anxiety and improve mood. Encouraging your teen to incorporate small amounts of physical activity into their daily routine can make a big difference in their overall mental health.

Incorporating physical activity and exercise into your teen's anxiety management plan can be a powerful tool for promoting mental well-being. By emphasizing the importance of staying active, supporting your teen in finding activities they enjoy, and modeling healthy behaviors, you can help your teen build resilience, reduce anxiety, and improve their overall quality of life. Remember, it's never too late to start incorporating physical activity into your routine – the benefits are endless!

Chapter 4: Building a Support System

Talking to Trusted Adults

One of the most important tools in managing anxiety as a teen is having open and honest conversations with trusted adults in your life. Whether it's a parent, teacher, school counselor, or family friend, having someone to confide in can make a world of difference. These adults can provide guidance, support, and valuable perspective on your struggles with anxiety.

When talking to trusted adults about your anxiety, it's important to be open and honest about how you're feeling. Expressing your thoughts and emotions can help you process them and gain a better understanding of what triggers your anxiety. Remember, these adults are there to help you, so don't be afraid to share your struggles with them.

Trusted adults can also offer practical advice on how to manage your anxiety. They may suggest relaxation techniques, breathing exercises, or other coping strategies that can help you calm your mind and body when you're feeling overwhelmed. Additionally, they can help you identify any patterns or triggers that may be contributing to your anxiety and work with you to develop a plan for managing these challenges.

In some cases, talking to a trusted adult may lead to seeking professional help for your anxiety. This could involve therapy, counseling, or medication, depending on the severity of your symptoms. Remember, it's okay to ask for help and take steps to improve your mental health. Your trusted adults are there to support you every step of the way.

Overall, talking to trusted adults about your anxiety can be a crucial step in managing your mental health. By opening up to someone you trust, you can gain valuable support, guidance, and resources to help you navigate your anxiety and build a more calm and confident life. Don't be afraid to reach out and start the conversation – you're not alone in this journey.

Connecting with Peers

In this subchapter, we will explore the importance of connecting with peers in managing anxiety. As teenagers, it is normal to feel overwhelmed by the pressures of school, relationships, and other responsibilities. However, having a strong support system of friends can make a huge difference in how we cope with these challenges. By building connections with our peers, we can feel less alone in our struggles and gain valuable insights and perspectives on how to navigate anxiety.

One of the key benefits of connecting with peers is that it can help us feel understood and validated. When we share our feelings and experiences with friends who are going through similar struggles, we realize that we are not alone in our anxiety. This sense of camaraderie can provide a sense of relief and comfort, knowing that there are others who truly understand what we are going through. By opening up to our peers, we can also receive valuable feedback and support that can help us manage our anxiety more effectively.

In addition to feeling understood, connecting with peers can also help us gain new perspectives on our anxiety. Our friends may offer insights and advice that we have not considered before, helping us see our situation from a different angle. By discussing our anxiety with others, we can learn new coping strategies and techniques that have worked for them. This exchange of ideas can be incredibly valuable in helping us develop a personalized approach to managing our anxiety.

Furthermore, building connections with peers can help us feel more supported and less isolated in our struggles. Knowing that we have friends who will listen to us without judgment and offer a shoulder to lean on can provide a sense of security and reassurance. This support system can be especially crucial during times of high stress or anxiety, as we can rely on our friends to help us through difficult moments. By nurturing these relationships, we can create a strong foundation of support that can help us weather any storm.

In conclusion, connecting with peers is a valuable tool in managing anxiety as a teenager. By sharing our feelings and experiences with friends, we can feel understood and validated, gain new perspectives on our anxiety, and build a support system that can help us navigate the challenges of adolescence. It is important to prioritize building and maintaining these connections, as they can play a crucial role in our overall mental health and well-being. Remember, you are not alone in your struggles – reaching out to your peers can make a world of difference in how you manage your anxiety.

Seeking Professional Help

For many teens struggling with anxiety, seeking professional help can be a daunting and intimidating step. However, it is important to remember that seeking help is a sign of strength and courage, not weakness. In fact, reaching out to a therapist or counselor can be a crucial first step towards managing anxiety and improving overall mental well-being.

One of the key benefits of seeking professional help is gaining access to specialized tools and techniques for managing anxiety. Therapists and counselors are trained to help individuals develop coping strategies and skills to better navigate challenging situations and emotions. Through therapy, teens can learn how to identify and challenge negative thought patterns, practice relaxation techniques, and build resilience in the face of stress.

Additionally, therapy provides a safe and confidential space for teens to explore their thoughts and feelings without fear of judgment. It can be incredibly empowering to have a supportive professional who listens without bias and offers guidance and support. By opening up to a therapist, teens can gain a deeper understanding of their anxiety triggers and develop personalized strategies for managing their symptoms.

Parents play a crucial role in supporting their teens in seeking professional help for anxiety. It is important for parents to validate their teen's feelings and experiences, and to encourage them to reach out for support when needed. By normalizing therapy and emphasizing its benefits, parents can help reduce the stigma surrounding mental health treatment and create a more open and supportive environment for their teen.

In conclusion, seeking professional help is a positive and proactive step towards managing anxiety and improving overall well-being. Therapy can provide teens with the tools, support, and guidance they need to navigate their anxiety and build resilience. By working with a therapist or counselor, teens can gain valuable insights, develop coping skills, and cultivate a greater sense of calm and confidence in their lives.

Chapter 5: Creating a Calm Environment

Organizing Your Space

One of the most important aspects of managing anxiety is creating a calm and organized environment in which to live and work. When our physical space is cluttered and chaotic, it can exacerbate feelings of stress and overwhelm. By taking the time to organize your space, you can create a sense of calm and order that will help to reduce anxiety levels.

Start by decluttering your space. Go through your belongings and get rid of anything that you no longer need or use. This will help to create more physical space in your environment, as well as reduce the mental clutter that comes with having too many possessions. Consider donating items to charity or selling them online to clear out your space and make room for things that truly matter to you.

Once you have decluttered, it's time to organize your remaining belongings. Invest in storage solutions such as bins, baskets, and shelves to help keep your space tidy and organized. Designate specific areas for different types of items, such as a basket for keys and wallets near the door, or a shelf for books and school supplies. By assigning each item a specific place, you can easily find what you need when you need it, reducing feelings of stress and anxiety.

In addition to physical organization, it's important to create a calming atmosphere in your space. Consider incorporating elements such as soft lighting, soothing colors, and natural elements like plants or flowers. These elements can help to create a peaceful and relaxing environment that can help to reduce anxiety levels. Consider adding a cozy blanket or pillow to your space to create a sense of comfort and security.

Finally, make sure to maintain your organized space on a regular basis. Set aside time each week to tidy up and put things back in their designated places. By staying on top of clutter and mess, you can prevent feelings of overwhelm and anxiety from building up. Remember, a tidy space leads to a tidy mind, so take the time to organize your space and create a calm and confident environment for yourself.

Creating a Relaxation Routine

Creating a relaxation routine is essential for managing anxiety and stress in your daily life. By incorporating regular relaxation practices into your routine, you can help calm your mind and body, leading to a greater sense of calm and confidence. This subchapter will explore different techniques and strategies that can help you create a relaxation routine that works for you.

One effective way to start your relaxation routine is by practicing deep breathing exercises. Deep breathing can help slow down your heart rate, relax your muscles, and calm your mind. Try taking slow, deep breaths in through your nose, holding for a few seconds, and then exhaling slowly through your mouth. Repeat this process several times to help center yourself and reduce feelings of anxiety.

Another important aspect of creating a relaxation routine is finding activities that bring you joy and relaxation. Whether it's listening to music, reading a book, going for a walk in nature, or practicing yoga, finding activities that help you unwind and relax can be a great way to manage anxiety. Make time in your schedule for these activities and prioritize self-care to help maintain a sense of calm and balance in your life.

In addition to relaxation techniques, it's important to also focus on maintaining a healthy lifestyle to help manage anxiety. Eating a balanced diet, getting regular exercise, and prioritizing sleep can all help reduce feelings of stress and anxiety. By taking care of your physical health, you can also support your mental well-being and create a solid foundation for managing anxiety.

Overall, creating a relaxation routine is a key component of managing anxiety as a teen. By incorporating deep breathing exercises, finding activities that bring you joy, and focusing on maintaining a healthy lifestyle, you can cultivate a sense of calm and confidence in your daily life. Remember that relaxation is a practice that takes time and effort, so be patient with yourself as you explore different techniques and find what works best for you.

Finding Hobbies and Activities that Bring Joy

One of the most important aspects of managing anxiety as a teen is finding hobbies and activities that bring you joy. When you are engaged in activities that you love, it can help to distract you from anxious thoughts and reduce stress levels. Whether it's painting, playing a musical instrument, or playing sports, finding what you enjoy can be a great way to cope with anxiety.

Parents can play a crucial role in helping their teen find hobbies and activities that bring them joy. Encouraging your teen to try new things and explore different interests can help them discover what they are passionate about. It's important for parents to be supportive and open-minded when it comes to their teen's hobbies, even if they may not understand or appreciate them themselves.

Teens, on the other hand, should not be afraid to experiment and try new things. It's okay to have a variety of interests and hobbies, as long as they bring you happiness and a sense of fulfillment. Don't be afraid to step out of your comfort zone and try something new – you may discover a hidden talent or passion that can help you manage your anxiety in a healthy way.

Finding hobbies and activities that bring you joy can also help you build self-confidence and self-esteem. When you excel at something you love, it can boost your mood and make you feel more capable and competent. This can be especially important for teens who struggle with anxiety, as it can help them feel more in control and confident in themselves.

Overall, finding hobbies and activities that bring joy is an essential part of managing anxiety as a teen. Whether it's through creative expression, physical activity, or socializing with friends, finding what makes you happy can have a positive impact on your mental health. By exploring different interests and passions, teens can find healthy ways to cope with anxiety and build resilience for the challenges ahead.

Chapter 6: Overcoming Challenges

Facing Fear and Avoidance

One of the biggest challenges in managing anxiety is facing fear and avoiding avoidance. It's natural to want to avoid things that make us anxious, but the more we avoid them, the stronger our anxiety becomes. This cycle can be difficult to break, but it is essential to overcome anxiety and regain control of our lives.

When we face our fears, we are able to confront them head-on and show ourselves that we are capable of handling the situation. This can help to build confidence and reduce anxiety over time. Avoiding avoidance means taking small steps towards facing our fears, even if it feels uncomfortable or scary. By gradually exposing ourselves to what makes us anxious, we can learn to manage our anxiety and become more resilient in the face of challenges.

It's important to remember that facing fear and avoiding avoidance is a process that takes time and patience. It's okay to feel scared or anxious when confronting our fears, but it's important to push through those feelings and continue moving forward. Seeking support from a therapist, counselor, or trusted adult can also be helpful in navigating this process and developing healthy coping strategies.

For teens, facing fear and avoiding avoidance can be especially challenging, as they may be dealing with a range of social, academic, and personal pressures. It's important for parents to support their teens in this process by providing encouragement, understanding, and guidance. By helping teens identify their fears and develop a plan for facing them, parents can empower their teens to overcome anxiety and build resilience.

In the end, facing fear and avoiding avoidance is a crucial step in managing anxiety and living a calm and confident life. By taking small steps towards confronting our fears, seeking support when needed, and staying committed to the process, we can overcome anxiety and regain control of our lives. Remember, you are not alone in this journey, and with the right tools and support, you can conquer your fears and live a life free from anxiety.

Setting Realistic Goals

Setting realistic goals is an important aspect of managing anxiety in teens. When it comes to setting goals, it's crucial to be realistic about what you can achieve. It's easy to get caught up in wanting to do everything perfectly, but setting unrealistic goals can lead to feelings of failure and increased anxiety. Instead, focus on setting small, achievable goals that you can work towards over time.

One way to set realistic goals is to break them down into smaller, more manageable steps. For example, if your goal is to improve your grades in school, break it down into smaller tasks such as studying for a certain amount of time each day, completing homework assignments on time, and seeking help when needed. By breaking your goals down into smaller steps, you can track your progress and celebrate small victories along the way.

Another important aspect of setting realistic goals is to be flexible. Life is unpredictable, and there will inevitably be obstacles that get in the way of achieving your goals. It's important to be flexible and willing to adjust your goals as needed. If you find that a goal is no longer realistic or achievable, it's okay to reassess and set a new goal that better fits your current circumstances.

It's also important to set goals that are meaningful to you. While it's great to have external motivators such as pleasing your parents or teachers, it's essential to set goals that align with your values and interests. When your goals are meaningful to you, you're more likely to stay motivated and focused on achieving them.

In conclusion, setting realistic goals is a key component of managing anxiety in teens. By breaking your goals down into smaller steps, being flexible, and setting goals that are meaningful to you, you can increase your chances of success and reduce feelings of anxiety. Remember to be patient with yourself and celebrate your progress along the way. Setting realistic goals is a skill that takes practice, but with time and effort, you can learn to set goals that are achievable and fulfilling.

Celebrating Successes and Progress

In the journey of managing anxiety, it's important to take the time to acknowledge and celebrate your successes and progress. It can be easy to get caught up in the day-to-day struggles and setbacks, but it's equally important to recognize the victories, no matter how small they may seem. By celebrating your successes, you can boost your confidence and motivation to continue working towards managing your anxiety effectively.

One way to celebrate your successes is to keep a journal or diary where you can track your progress. Write down the goals you have achieved, the moments when you felt proud of yourself, and the steps you have taken towards managing your anxiety. By reflecting on your journey in this way, you can see how far you have come and remind yourself of the progress you have made.

Another way to celebrate your successes is to share them with others. Whether it's with a trusted friend, family member, or therapist, talking about your achievements can help reinforce the positive changes you are making in managing your anxiety. By sharing your successes, you can also receive encouragement and support from those around you, which can be incredibly motivating.

As a parent, it's important to recognize and celebrate your teen's successes and progress in managing their anxiety. Be sure to acknowledge their efforts and achievements, and offer words of encouragement and support. Celebrating your teen's successes can help boost their confidence and self-esteem, as well as strengthen your relationship with them.

Overall, celebrating successes and progress is an important part of managing anxiety. By acknowledging your achievements, tracking your progress, sharing your successes with others, and receiving support from those around you, you can stay motivated and confident in your ability to overcome anxiety. Remember, every step forward is worth celebrating, no matter how small it may seem.

Chapter 7: Maintaining a Calm and Confident Mindset

Practicing Self-Compassion

Practicing self-compassion is an essential tool in managing anxiety. It involves treating yourself with kindness and understanding, especially during times when you may be feeling overwhelmed or stressed. As a teen, it's easy to be hard on yourself and set high expectations that can lead to feelings of inadequacy. By practicing self-compassion, you can learn to be more forgiving and accepting of yourself, which can help reduce anxiety and improve your overall well-being.

One way to practice self-compassion is by being mindful of your thoughts and emotions. When you notice yourself being self-critical or judgmental, try to reframe those thoughts with kindness and understanding. For example, instead of saying "I'm such a failure," try saying "I made a mistake, but everyone makes mistakes and it's okay." By changing the way you talk to yourself, you can cultivate a more positive and compassionate inner dialogue.

Another way to practice self-compassion is by taking care of yourself physically and emotionally. This means making time for activities that bring you joy and relaxation, such as exercise, hobbies, or spending time with friends. It also means being gentle with yourself when you're feeling stressed or anxious, and giving yourself permission to take breaks when needed. Remember, it's okay to prioritize your own well-being and set boundaries with others when necessary.

Practicing self-compassion can also involve seeking support from others, such as friends, family, or a therapist. Talking about your feelings and experiences can help you feel less alone and more understood, which can in turn reduce feelings of anxiety and improve your mental health. Remember, it's not a sign of weakness to ask for help when you need it – in fact, it takes courage and strength to reach out and seek support.

In conclusion, practicing self-compassion is a powerful tool in managing anxiety as a teen. By being kind and understanding towards yourself, taking care of your physical and emotional well-being, and seeking support when needed, you can cultivate a more positive and resilient mindset that can help you navigate the challenges of adolescence with greater ease and confidence. Remember, you deserve to treat yourself with the same compassion and care that you would offer to a friend in need.

Developing Positive Self-Talk

Developing positive self-talk is an essential tool in managing anxiety and building confidence. The way we talk to ourselves has a significant impact on our mental health and well-being. Negative self-talk can fuel anxiety and self-doubt, while positive self-talk can foster a sense of calm and self-assurance. In this subchapter, we will explore strategies for developing positive self-talk and incorporating it into your daily routine.

One way to develop positive self-talk is to challenge negative thoughts and replace them with more realistic and positive ones. For example, if you catch yourself thinking "I'm not good enough" or "I'll never succeed," challenge those thoughts by asking yourself for evidence to support them. More often than not, you will find that these negative beliefs are not based on facts but on fear and self-doubt. Replace those thoughts with affirmations such as "I am capable and deserving of success" or "I have the skills and resources to overcome challenges."

Another helpful strategy for developing positive self-talk is to practice self-compassion. Treat yourself with the same kindness and understanding that you would offer a friend facing a difficult situation. Instead of berating yourself for making mistakes or not measuring up to your own expectations, acknowledge your humanity and imperfections. Remind yourself that it's okay to make mistakes and that you are worthy of love and acceptance just as you are.

Incorporating mindfulness into your daily routine can also help cultivate positive self-talk. Mindfulness involves being present in the moment and observing your thoughts and feelings without judgment. By practicing mindfulness, you can become more aware of negative self-talk patterns and learn to let go of unhelpful thoughts. Instead of getting caught up in a spiral of self-criticism, you can choose to redirect your focus to the present moment and cultivate a sense of calm and acceptance.

Lastly, seeking support from trusted friends, family members, or a mental health professional can be invaluable in developing positive self-talk. Talking openly about your struggles and receiving validation and encouragement from others can help challenge negative beliefs and build confidence. Surrounding yourself with a supportive network of people who believe in you and your abilities can reinforce positive self-talk and help you navigate challenging situations with greater ease.

In conclusion, developing positive self-talk is a powerful tool in managing anxiety and building confidence. By challenging negative thoughts, practicing self-compassion, incorporating mindfulness, and seeking support, you can cultivate a more positive and empowering inner dialogue. Remember that changing long-standing patterns of negative self-talk takes time and effort, but with persistence and self-compassion, you can transform the way you talk to yourself and cultivate a sense of calm and confidence.

Finding Balance in Your Life

Finding balance in your life is crucial when it comes to managing anxiety. As a teen, it can be challenging to juggle school, extracurricular activities, social life, and family obligations. However, finding a balance between all these aspects of your life is essential for maintaining your mental health and well-being.

One way to find balance in your life is to prioritize your commitments and responsibilities. It's important to understand that you can't do everything, and that's okay. Learn to say no to things that don't align with your values or goals, and focus on the activities that truly matter to you. By prioritizing your time and energy, you can create a more balanced schedule that allows you to take care of yourself while still meeting your obligations.

Another way to find balance in your life is to make time for self-care. Self-care activities, such as exercise, meditation, journaling, or spending time with loved ones, can help you relax, recharge, and reduce stress. By incorporating self-care into your daily routine, you can better manage your anxiety and maintain a sense of balance in your life.

Communication is also key to finding balance in your life. Talk to your parents, teachers, or friends about how you're feeling and what you need. By expressing your thoughts and emotions, you can receive support and guidance from others, which can help you navigate the challenges of balancing your responsibilities and managing your anxiety.

Lastly, remember that finding balance is an ongoing process. It's normal to feel overwhelmed at times, but by practicing self-awareness, setting boundaries, and seeking support when needed, you can create a more balanced and fulfilling life. By taking care of yourself and prioritizing your well-being, you can better manage your anxiety and thrive as a teen.

Chapter 8: Supporting Your Teen Through Anxiety

Communicating with Your Teen

Effective communication is key when it comes to managing anxiety as a teenager. As a parent, it can be challenging to understand what your teen is going through, and as a teen, it can be difficult to express your feelings and concerns. However, open and honest communication is essential in helping both parties navigate the challenges of anxiety.

As a teenager, it's important to remember that your parents are there to support you. They may not always understand what you're going through, but by communicating openly with them, you can help them understand your struggles and provide the necessary support. When talking to your parents about your anxiety, be honest about how you're feeling and what you need from them. This can help strengthen your relationship and build trust between you and your parents.

Parents, on the other hand, should create a safe and supportive environment for their teens to communicate. Listen actively to what your teen has to say without judgment or criticism. Encourage them to express their feelings and thoughts, and validate their emotions. By being a supportive and understanding presence in your teen's life, you can help them feel comfortable opening up about their anxiety and seeking help when needed.

When communicating with your teen about anxiety, it's important to use language that is clear and simple. Avoid using complicated or technical terms that may confuse them. Instead, focus on expressing your thoughts and feelings in a way that is easy for them to understand. By communicating clearly, you can ensure that both you and your teen are on the same page when it comes to managing anxiety.

Overall, effective communication is essential in helping teens manage anxiety. By fostering open and honest communication between parents and teens, both parties can work together to address anxiety and find solutions that work for everyone involved. Remember to be patient, understanding, and supportive when communicating with your teen about anxiety, and always prioritize their well-being above all else.

Encouraging Healthy Habits

It is important for teens to establish healthy habits in order to manage anxiety effectively. One of the most crucial habits to develop is regular exercise. Physical activity has been shown to reduce symptoms of anxiety and improve overall mental health. Encourage your teen to find a form of exercise that they enjoy, whether it be going for a run, practicing yoga, or playing a team sport. Not only will exercise help to alleviate anxiety, but it will also boost their mood and increase their self-confidence.

In addition to exercise, maintaining a balanced diet is essential for managing anxiety. Encourage your teen to eat a variety of nutritious foods, including fruits, vegetables, whole grains, and lean proteins. Avoiding excessive consumption of caffeine, sugar, and processed foods can also help to regulate mood and reduce anxiety. Encourage your teen to stay hydrated by drinking plenty of water throughout the day. A well-nourished body is better equipped to cope with stress and anxiety.

Another healthy habit that can benefit teens struggling with anxiety is getting an adequate amount of sleep. Lack of sleep can exacerbate feelings of anxiety and make it more difficult to cope with stress. Encourage your teen to establish a bedtime routine that allows for at least 8-9 hours of quality sleep each night. Limiting screen time before bed, creating a relaxing environment, and practicing relaxation techniques can all help to promote better sleep habits.

It is also important for teens to establish healthy coping mechanisms for managing anxiety. Encourage your teen to practice mindfulness and relaxation techniques, such as deep breathing exercises and meditation. Journaling can also be a helpful way for teens to express their feelings and process their emotions. Encourage your teen to reach out for support when needed, whether it be from a trusted friend, family member, or mental health professional. Building a strong support network can help teens feel less alone in their struggles with anxiety.

Overall, encouraging healthy habits is crucial for teens to effectively manage their anxiety. By promoting regular exercise, a balanced diet, quality sleep, and healthy coping mechanisms, you can help your teen develop the resilience and strength needed to navigate the challenges of anxiety. Encourage open communication and provide a supportive environment for your teen to explore different strategies for managing their anxiety. With the right tools and support, teens can learn to calm their minds and build confidence in their ability to cope with anxiety.

Seeking Professional Guidance

Seeking professional guidance can be a crucial step in managing anxiety. While it may be intimidating to reach out for help, speaking with a therapist or counselor can provide you with the tools and support you need to navigate your anxiety. These professionals are trained to help individuals work through their emotions, develop coping strategies, and identify triggers that may be contributing to their anxiety. By seeking professional guidance, you are taking an important step towards taking control of your mental health.

Teens and parents should not hesitate to seek out a therapist or counselor if they are struggling with anxiety. These professionals can offer a safe space for teens to talk about their feelings and experiences without fear of judgment. They can also provide valuable insights and strategies for managing anxiety in a healthy and effective way. Additionally, therapists and counselors can work with parents to help them better understand their teen's anxiety and provide support and guidance for both the teen and the family as a whole.

When seeking professional guidance for anxiety, it is important to find a therapist or counselor who specializes in working with teens. These professionals will have a better understanding of the unique challenges that adolescents face and will be better equipped to provide targeted support and interventions. It may also be helpful to seek out a therapist who uses evidence-based treatments, such as cognitive-behavioral therapy (CBT), which has been shown to be effective in treating anxiety disorders in teens.

In addition to therapy, there are other forms of professional guidance that can be beneficial for teens struggling with anxiety. Psychiatrists can prescribe medication to help manage anxiety symptoms, while school counselors can provide support and resources for teens dealing with anxiety in an academic setting. Whatever form of professional guidance you choose, remember that you are not alone in your struggles and that there are people who are trained and ready to help you work through your anxiety in a healthy and productive way.

Overall, seeking professional guidance is an important step in managing anxiety. By reaching out for help, you are taking control of your mental health and working towards a happier and more confident future. Remember that it is okay to ask for help, and that there are professionals who are ready and willing to support you on your journey towards managing anxiety.

Chapter 9: Resources for Further Support

Hotlines and Helplines

Hotlines and helplines can be valuable resources for teens struggling with anxiety. These services provide a confidential and nonjudgmental space for individuals to talk about their feelings and receive support. Whether you're feeling overwhelmed with schoolwork, experiencing social anxiety, or just need someone to talk to, hotlines and helplines are there to help.

One popular hotline for teens is the Crisis Text Line, which allows individuals to text trained crisis counselors for support. This service is available 24/7 and is completely confidential. Another option is the National Suicide Prevention Lifeline, which provides support for individuals experiencing suicidal thoughts or feelings of hopelessness. These hotlines offer a safe space for teens to express their emotions and receive guidance on how to cope with their anxiety.

Parents can also benefit from hotlines and helplines when they are unsure how to support their anxious teen. The Parent Helpline, run by the National Alliance on Mental Illness (NAMI), offers support and resources for parents struggling to understand their child's anxiety. By reaching out to these services, parents can gain valuable insights on how to best support their teen through their anxiety struggles.

It's important for both teens and parents to be aware of the hotlines and helplines available to them. These resources can provide a lifeline during moments of crisis and offer ongoing support for managing anxiety. By utilizing these services, teens can learn healthy coping mechanisms and parents can gain the tools they need to support their anxious child effectively.

In conclusion, hotlines and helplines are valuable resources for teens and parents navigating the challenges of anxiety. By reaching out for help, individuals can find the support they need to manage their anxiety and improve their mental well-being. Remember, you are not alone in your struggles, and help is just a phone call or text away.

Online Support Groups

In today's digital age, online support groups have become a valuable resource for teens struggling with anxiety. These virtual communities provide a safe space for individuals to share their experiences, seek advice, and connect with others who are facing similar challenges. By joining an online support group, teens can find comfort in knowing they are not alone in their struggles.

One of the key benefits of online support groups is the accessibility they offer. Teens can participate in discussions and seek support from the comfort of their own homes, eliminating the barriers that may prevent them from seeking help in person. This can be especially beneficial for teens who may feel anxious about attending traditional support groups or therapy sessions.

Online support groups also provide a sense of anonymity, which can be empowering for teens who may feel reluctant to share their struggles with friends or family members. By interacting with others online, teens can express themselves freely and openly without fear of judgment. This can help teens build confidence and develop coping strategies for managing their anxiety.

Additionally, online support groups can provide valuable resources and information to help teens better understand and manage their anxiety. Many groups offer tips, tools, and techniques for coping with anxiety, as well as recommendations for seeking professional help if needed. By engaging with these resources, teens can develop a better understanding of their anxiety and learn how to effectively manage it.

Overall, online support groups can be a valuable tool for teens struggling with anxiety. By connecting with others who understand their struggles, teens can find comfort, support, and valuable resources to help them navigate their anxiety. Whether seeking advice, sharing experiences, or simply connecting with others, online support groups can play a crucial role in helping teens manage their anxiety and build a sense of calm and confidence.

Books and Websites for Additional Information

For teens and parents looking for more resources on managing anxiety, there are numerous books and websites available that provide valuable information and support. These resources can offer strategies, tips, and insights into how to cope with anxiety and build resilience. Here are some recommendations for books and websites that can help teens navigate their anxiety in a healthy and productive way.

One highly recommended book for teens struggling with anxiety is "The Anxiety Workbook for Teens" by Lisa Schab. This workbook provides practical exercises and techniques for managing anxiety, including mindfulness practices and cognitive behavioral therapy strategies. It also offers guidance on how to identify triggers and develop coping skills to reduce anxiety levels. This book can be a helpful tool for teens looking to take control of their anxiety and improve their mental well-being.

Another valuable resource is the Anxiety and Depression Association of America (ADAA) website. This website offers a wealth of information on anxiety disorders, including articles, webinars, and resources for teens and parents. The ADAA website also provides a directory of mental health professionals and support groups for those seeking additional help. By exploring this website, teens can gain a better understanding of anxiety and access valuable resources to support their mental health journey.

For parents looking to better understand and support their teens with anxiety, the book "The Anxiety and Phobia Workbook" by Edmund J. Bourne, PhD, is a great resource. This comprehensive guide offers insights into the causes of anxiety, as well as practical strategies for helping teens manage their symptoms. The book covers a range of anxiety disorders, including social anxiety, panic attacks, and phobias, and provides tools for parents to communicate effectively with their teens about their struggles.

In addition to books and websites, online platforms such as AnxietyBC and ReachOut can also be valuable resources for teens seeking support and information on managing anxiety. These websites offer articles, videos, and tools to help teens understand and cope with anxiety, as well as access to mental health professionals and peer support networks. By exploring these online platforms, teens can find a sense of community and learn new strategies for managing their anxiety in a healthy way.

Overall, books and websites can be valuable tools for teens and parents seeking additional information and support for managing anxiety. By exploring these resources, teens can gain insights into their anxiety, develop coping skills, and build resilience to navigate life's challenges with confidence and calm. Remember, you are not alone in your struggles, and there are resources available to help you on your journey to managing anxiety effectively.

Chapter 10: Moving Forward with Confidence

Setting Long-Term Goals

Setting long-term goals is an important aspect of managing anxiety as a teen. When you have a clear vision of where you want to be in the future, it can help alleviate feelings of uncertainty and stress. By setting long-term goals, you are giving yourself something to work towards and a sense of purpose in your life. This can help boost your confidence and motivation, which are essential in overcoming anxiety.

One important thing to remember when setting long-term goals is to make sure they are realistic and achievable. It's great to have big dreams, but it's also important to break them down into smaller, more manageable steps. This can help prevent feelings of overwhelm and ensure that you are making progress towards your goals. By setting achievable goals, you are setting yourself up for success and building a strong foundation for managing your anxiety.

Another key aspect of setting long-term goals is to make sure they are specific and measurable. Vague goals like "be successful" or "be happy" can be difficult to track and accomplish. Instead, try setting goals like "graduate from college with a degree in psychology" or "run a marathon in under four hours." These specific goals give you a clear target to aim for and a way to measure your progress along the way.

It's also important to revisit your long-term goals regularly and make adjustments as needed. As you grow and change, your goals may need to evolve as well. Don't be afraid to reassess your goals and make changes if necessary. This flexibility can help you stay on track and ensure that your goals continue to align with your values and aspirations.

In conclusion, setting long-term goals is an essential tool in managing anxiety as a teen. By establishing realistic, specific, and measurable goals, you can give yourself a sense of direction and purpose. Remember to break your goals down into smaller steps, revisit them regularly, and make adjustments as needed. With a clear vision of your future and a plan to get there, you can build confidence, motivation, and resilience in the face of anxiety.

Reflecting on Progress

Reflecting on progress is an important aspect of managing anxiety as a teen. It allows us to see how far we have come in our journey towards calming our minds and feeling more confident in ourselves. Taking the time to reflect on our progress can provide us with a sense of accomplishment and motivation to continue working towards our goals. This subchapter will explore the benefits of reflecting on progress and provide tips on how to effectively do so.

One of the benefits of reflecting on progress is that it allows us to see the positive changes we have made in managing our anxiety. By looking back on where we started and comparing it to where we are now, we can see the progress we have made in terms of our thoughts, feelings, and behaviors. This can help boost our confidence and self-esteem, as we realize that we are capable of overcoming challenges and making positive changes in our lives.

Reflecting on progress also helps us to identify what strategies have been most effective in managing our anxiety. By looking back on our journey, we can see which techniques have worked well for us and which ones may need to be adjusted or replaced. This can help us to fine-tune our anxiety management skills and develop a more personalized approach that works best for us. It also allows us to celebrate our successes and acknowledge the hard work we have put in to make positive changes in our lives.

In order to effectively reflect on progress, it is important to set aside dedicated time for self-reflection. This can involve journaling about our thoughts and feelings, talking with a trusted friend or family member about our progress, or simply taking a few moments each day to think about how far we have come. It is also helpful to set specific goals for ourselves and track our progress towards achieving them. This can provide us with a sense of direction and purpose, as well as a roadmap for where we want to go in our anxiety management journey.

As teens, it is also important to involve our parents in our reflection on progress. They can provide valuable insight and support as we navigate the ups and downs of managing anxiety. By sharing our successes and challenges with our parents, we can strengthen our bond with them and receive the guidance and encouragement we need to continue moving forward. Reflecting on progress together can also help us to set realistic expectations and celebrate our achievements as a team. By working together, teens and parents can create a supportive environment that fosters growth, resilience, and confidence in managing anxiety.

Embracing a Future with Less Anxiety

In this subchapter, we will discuss the importance of embracing a future with less anxiety. As a teenager, it is common to feel overwhelmed by the pressures of school, relationships, and future uncertainties. However, by learning how to manage anxiety effectively, you can take control of your emotions and create a more peaceful and fulfilling future for yourself.

One of the first steps in embracing a future with less anxiety is to identify the sources of your stress and anxiety. By understanding what triggers your anxious thoughts and feelings, you can begin to address them head-on. This may involve talking to a trusted adult, seeking therapy, or practicing relaxation techniques such as deep breathing or meditation.

It is also important to remember that you are not alone in your struggles with anxiety. Many teenagers experience similar feelings of fear and worry, and it is okay to reach out for help when you need it. By talking to friends, family members, or mental health professionals, you can gain valuable support and guidance in managing your anxiety.

Another key aspect of embracing a future with less anxiety is to focus on the present moment. Instead of worrying about what may happen in the future, try to stay grounded in the here and now. Practice mindfulness techniques such as journaling, yoga, or simply taking a walk outside to help calm your mind and reduce anxiety.

By taking proactive steps to manage your anxiety and embrace a future with less stress, you can build confidence and resilience that will serve you well throughout your teenage years and beyond. Remember, it is okay to ask for help when you need it, and by prioritizing your mental health, you can create a brighter and more peaceful future for yourself.

Perry Clement

I am so pleased to write these guides for young people and their parents who wish to improve their overall mental health.

As a professional working with young people for over 20 years I have seen the effects of anxiety and other mental health conditions on young people and their parents. To manage and stay on top of your mental health takes time, effort and work.

I encourage everyone to read, investigate and seek a therapist that you can relate to and get the most out of.

To contact me and make a booking for help with your anxiety, depression, PTSD, autism or any mental health related condition or social skills development please contact me on mentalhealthshops@gmail.com.

Good luck and stay well.

Mental Health Matters! #mentalhealthmatters join the movement today!

https://mentalhealthmat.etsy.com